D0708858

BOOKS BY TED KOOSER

Available from the University of Nebraska Press

The Blizzard Voices

Local Wonders

The Poetry Home Repair Manual

Valentines

Writing Brave and Free

Lights on a Ground of Darkness

AN EVOCATION OF A PLACE AND TIME

TED KOOSER

University of Nebraska Press
Lincoln & London

⊗

A special limited edition of this
volume was first published in cloth
by the University of Nebraska Press
in 2005. First paperback printing:
2009.

Photographs courtesy of the author.

Library of Congress Cataloging-in-
Publication Data

Kooser, Ted. Lights on a ground of
darkness : an evocation of a place and
time / Ted Kooser.
    p. cm.
ISBN 978-0-8032-2642-5 (pbk. : alk.
paper)
1. Kooser, Ted—Childhood and
youth. 2. Kooser, Ted—Homes and
haunts—Iowa. 3. Kooser, Ted—
Family. 4. Poets, American—20th
century—Biography. 5. Iowa—Social
life and customs. I. Title.
PS3561.O6Z465 2009
811′.54—dc22
[B]
2009007721

Designed and set in Minion
by Roger D. Buchholz

To the memory of my mother,
Vera Deloras Moser Kooser,
August 25, 1908–March 23, 1998

Mid April already, and the wild plums
bloom at the roadside, a lacy white
against the exuberant, jubilant green
of new grass and the dusty, fading black
of burned-out ditches. No leaves, not yet,
only the delicate, star-petaled
blossoms, sweet with their timeless perfume.

You have been gone a month today
and have missed three rains and one nightlong
watch for tornados. I sat in the cellar
from six to eight while fat spring clouds
went somersaulting, rumbling east. Then it poured,
a storm that walked on legs of lightning,
dragging its shaggy belly over the fields.

The meadowlarks are back, and the finches
are turning from green to gold. Those same
two geese have come to the pond again this year,
honking in over the trees and splashing down.
They never nest, but stay a week or two
then leave. The peonies are up, the red sprouts
burning in circles like birthday candles,

for this is the month of my birth, as you know,
the best month to be born in, thanks to you,
everything ready to burst with living.
There will be no more new flannel nightshirts
sewn on your old black Singer, no birthday card
addressed in a shaky but businesslike hand.
You asked me if I would be sad when it happened

and I am sad. But the iris I moved from your house
now hold in the dusty dry fists of their roots
green knives and forks as if waiting for dinner,
as if spring were a feast. I thank you for that.
Were it not for the way you taught me to look
at the world, to see the life at play in everything,
I would have to be lonely forever.

John R. Moser, my grandfather

Vera Moser Kooser, my mother

Judy and Teddy Kooser

This is a book I put off writing for more than fifty years because I wanted it to be perfect, which it is not and could never be. In almost every family there is someone like me who desperately wants to write such a story and is forever kept from it by fear of failure.

From the time I was a little boy I dreamed of one day writing a marvelous book about my mother's family. My words, I thought, if ever they were to be written, would in splendor and beauty offer to the world the people I most loved, the family shining at the center of my heart. I would show the John R. Mosers as remarkable, heroic even, not just an ordinary handful of working-class German Americans crowded into a house next to a filling station on the edge of town.

In the autumn of 1997 it became clear that my mother would not live long. Her heart and lungs were failing, she was on oxygen day and night, she had moved into an assisted-living apartment, and she was preparing to die. She was the last living member of her family, and before she was gone I wanted to show her how much I had loved them.

I spent that autumn and winter urgently gathering my memories and writing them down, and two months before her death I gave her a copy of the manuscript. I was fearful that my words might make her sad at the sad end of her days, but I took the risk. She read it and, much to my relief, she told me that she liked what I had done.

It did not see publication until after her death, when it appeared in an issue of *Great River Review*, a Minnesota literary quarterly. I am grateful to the editors there for giving me the first opportunity to present my words to readers other than my mother, there in her chair by the window, looking out at the last of her eighty-nine years.

Those of you who know my *Local Wonders: Seasons in the Bohemian Alps* (University of Nebraska Press, 2003), will recognize the description of my father's hands, which first appeared in this essay. And the poem for my mother, which opens this book, appears in my collection of verse, *Delights & Shadows* (Copper Canyon Press, 2004). I am grateful to the University of Nebraska Press for making so handsome a package of these memories.

Ted Kooser
Garland, Nebraska
September 2004

Time wakens a longing more poignant than all the longings caused by the division of lovers in space, for there is no road back into its country. Our bodies were not made for that journey; only the imagination can venture upon it; and the setting out, the road, and the arrival: all is imagination.

Our memories of a place, no matter how fond we were of it, are little more than a confusion of lights on a ground of darkness.—Edwin Muir

Lights on a Ground of Darkness

AN EVOCATION OF A PLACE AND TIME

Summer, 1949. Above the Mississippi, the noon sun bleaches the blue from a cloudless midsummer sky. So high in their flight that they might be no more than tiny motes afloat on the surface of the eye, a few cliff swallows dive and roll. At the base of the shadowy bluffs a highway weaves through the valley, its surface shimmering like a field of wheat; to the south, a semi loaded with squealing hogs shifts down for the slow crawl up out of the bottoms and into the bright, flat cornfields of eastern Iowa. The bitter odor of exhaust clings like spider webs to the long grass lining the shoulders of the road. Toward the top of the grade the sound of the engine levels out into a brash and steady saxophone note that rattles back through the cut, and then, with a fading whine, the truck is gone, leaving the hot road shining empty down the length of the valley.

The little town of Guttenberg, Iowa, is taking a midday nap under the trees on the bank of the river. Its wide streets are quiet, its window shades drawn down against the heat. Old elms sprinkle the deserted sidewalks with lacy, drifting patterns. There's a light breeze off the water, carrying the smell of fish and the soft, regular sound of waves lapping the sides of tied-up boats. In one back yard an old woman in a blue bathrobe and a wide-brimmed straw hat walks a plank pathway through her garden, inspecting the leaves of her beans with the tip of a cane.

Front Street, which in any other small town might be called Main Street, divides a shady riverbank park from a row of old store buildings. The Mississippi here is wide and smooth, pooled by a government lock and dam. Beyond the dark green channel islands, the bluffs of Wisconsin rise pale and vaporous. Far out, between two of the islands, a tug slowly pushes a long line of rusty coal barges north toward Minnesota. A few old men sit on shaded benches in the park, swapping stories and watching the river birds loop and skim over the water.

The buildings that face the river all date from the mid-1800s. Nearly all of them are two stories in height, built of cut limestone or of brick, with elaborate stone cornices. The original storefronts, with their high windows and recessed entryways, have been "modernized," but the original facades still peer over the tops of the glaring spreads of glass and the slick cummerbunds of new signs. You have to sit in the park and squint hard to see the town as it once was, a busy river port of the days of the big stern-wheelers, the fancy trim of its buildings mirroring the cut wooden gingerbread on the steamboats.

The businesses that line Front Street are those that

one expects to find in any small town. There's a hard-ware store, its windows full of red power mowers, green fertilizer spreaders, and blue bicycles. There's the BonTon Dress Shop, unabashedly showing last year's fashions on dazed and flaking mannequins. There's the Blackbird Variety, with a leaky pop case out front. There's a bakery and a Thom McAn shoe-store. There are a couple of buildings that once were stores but have since been converted into private residences, with curtains drawn across the dis-play windows and potted plants on the stoops. At the north end of the row of buildings sits the post office, plain as a peach crate. At its side, the draft from a window fan shakes a dead spirea bush. The American flag runs down its hot steel pole like candle wax.

The banks of every river are made of history. In 1763, Marquette and Joliet drifted past this place. "Now here we are on this beautiful river!" wrote Father Marquette, having left the smaller Wisconsin River behind him. Later, boatmen from downriver bartered cargoes of tools, powder, guns, and traps for furs from French trappers, who in turn traded with the Sac and Fox. Long before there were any buildings in the town, there were crude landing docks roped together out of rough-sawn boards. Traders camped on the riverbank, sleeping in tents made by throwing a blanket over a hemp rope stretched between two trees. Once, according to the two-volume county history, two of these men fought a duel with rattlesnakes held in their hands. Both survived. In the 1840s, an artist named Henry Lewis drifted past here on his longboat, and painted a panorama of the Mississippi, from the falls of St. Anthony to New Orleans, on a roll of canvas twelve feet high and 1,325 yards long. The canvas was meant to be slowly scrolled past the proscenium of a theater during a lecture. In the late 1800s, a few miles up the river, at McGregor, the talented young Ringling brothers were just getting started on their circus business by performing their tumbling and juggling act for people on the street.

On the south edge of this little town, past the empty mussel shell button factory and the lumberyard, past the abandoned creamery and a few trailer houses glinting in the sun, sits a red brick Standard Oil filling station and, near it, shaded by a tall catalpa, a white bungalow with a screened porch. The graveled driveway is lined with smooth boulders freshly whitewashed, and a neatly pruned hedge separates the front yard from the highway. On the porch, my grandmother, a thin, shy woman in her late sixties, carefully waters a huge fern in a wicker planter. There is a patch of irises next to the front stoop, yellow and salmon pink and blue, from roots that have been moved from house to house down the years.

In the yard behind the house, a wooden picnic table has been pulled up under a low-branching

Chinese elm, and my sister, Judy, who is seven, and I, ten, are playing "Swinging Off the Table." It's a game we have just invented, and it involves great daring and much squealing and laughter. Each in turn kicks off and swings away from the table on a low branch that slowly bends to set us down on the grass. Our only audience as we play is my grandmother's little flock of white leghorn hens, bunched together at our side of their pen, watching us as if we were something to eat. We are here during our annual two-week summer stay with our grandparents. Our mother is with us, somewhere in the house, and our father is two hundred miles away. He will be coming to take us all home when he is able to get away from his store.

～The roof of my grandfather's filling station extends out over the pumps, supported by two stout brick columns, and in the shade of this overhang my grandfather, a short, bald man in a blue Standard Oil uniform and matching cap, is giving my Uncle Elvy a shave. Elvy sits on a wooden folding chair with a towel wrapped around his shoulders, white lather on his chin, and a look of infinite patience on his big loose face. A station wagon with Illinois plates, driven by a harried-looking woman and packed with wrestling children, has pulled in off the highway, and my uncle must wait while my grandfather pumps gas and checks the oil and washes the windshield. The Illinois children press their faces to the car windows, gawking and making faces at the funny-looking man with soap on his face. Elvy looks back, smiling through the foam.

My Uncle Elvy is at the center of this scene and at the center of our love. He has cerebral palsy and is wholly dependent upon his parents and upon a community that accepts him as its own. When he is up from his folding chair and on his feet—walking to the well for a pail of drinking water or along the roadside, evenings, coming home from fishing, cane poles rattling over his shoulder—he moves with a stumbling, pigeon-toed gait. His tongue is thick and almost always out, and his chin is usually in need of wiping. He has such difficulty forming words that it takes years of listening to him before you can understand what he is saying. He has dentures but refuses to wear them because they hurt his mouth. Like his mother's family, the Morarends, he is painfully shy. When he speaks, fighting hard for every syllable, he lowers his eyes and his hair falls forward in a loose, dark lock. He has a sweet, guileless smile and is fond of children, reaching to touch them with a soft, moist, tentative hand.

He loves to fish and he fishes nearly every day, all summer long. He will go to the river this very afternoon, and I will help him dig worms in the chicken yard, Elvy clumsy with the dirt fork and I on my knees in the manure-spattered clay, fighting the hens for the fat, wet worms.

Below the government's lock and dam, the Mississippi meanders aimlessly through the muddy, overgrown bottomland, pooling in motionless sloughs and swilling up around hundreds of small, low islands covered by underbrush, driftwood, willows, and the stark white masts of dead cottonwoods.

The nearest backwater is less than a quarter-mile east of the house, across the narrow highway, the railroad tracks, and a strip of field corn that is troubled by too much water at the root and too many raccoons at the ear. Neither the slough nor the river beyond it can be seen from my grandparents' house, but the river continually declares its presence in the flights and cries of water birds and in the mournful lowing of riverboats pushing their strings of barges up the main channel.

The corn in that strip of bottomland belongs to another man, but my grandfather each summer chops a path through it for my uncle to follow to the river, a trail just wide enough to keep him from getting his fishpoles entangled as they thrash from side to side. If the owner of the land cares about the lost corn, he never complains. If it takes the loss of three or four rows of corn to get Elvy Moser down to the river and back, so be it.

When he returns at dusk, he will be dragging a gunnysack full of fish that leaves a wet slick along the shoulder like one made by a snail. He will turn into the yard and pour the sack on the grass for my grandmother to sort through. There are all sorts of fish in the slough, and he brings them all home because he has caught them and they are his: dogfish and gar, carp and buffalo and red horse, bullheads and channel cat, sunfish and bluegills. On the dark green, dewy grass of early evening, they shine like silver, a few of them still twisting, their sharp mouths gaping for air. We stand there slapping mosquitoes while my grandmother picks out several to clean for supper. Then she asks Elvy to throw the rest to the chickens, and my sister and I follow him to watch the hens as they fight over the fish.

༄ Not everyone is good to Elvy. One of the old men who come to the station every day is Carl Beck, a squat, red-faced man in his seventies. His bib overalls are bleached at the crotch and he wears a railroader's denim hat. He is mean to my uncle and teases him mercilessly when my grandfather is not within earshot. "When your folks die, Elvy, you'll have to go to a home," he says in a coarse whisper, "and they don't feed you good in them places. They beat you with a stick if you don't talk right." My uncle's only defense against Carl Beck is to avoid him whenever he can, and when Beck comes walking down the shoulder toward the station, Elvy gets up and heads for the house. A few years from now, when somebody brings the news that Carl Beck has been found dead in his trailer house, my uncle's face will break into a broad, wet smile.

⟶ Most of our evenings are quiet, spent on the screened porch talking, but tonight is to be pinochle night, and after a supper of fried bluegills and potatoes and canned peaches, we wait on the porch for the cardplayers to arrive. Grandmother is busy in the kitchen doing up the dishes and preparing the refreshments for later. On the porch, my grandfather and his youngest daughter, my mother, tell stories about friends and relatives, some of whom have moved far away or who have been dead for many years. Some of the stories are tinged with mystery, and I will carry them with me forever.

Tonight my mother mentions an afternoon visit, many years before, from a woman with elephantiasis, a cousin to a distant branch of the family who hadn't been back for many years. But the gossip about her disease and disfigurement had paid its regular visits along the back roads, and a great deal of anticipation preceded her high-topped buggy as it stopped at the sites of her youth. It was said that though as a girl she had been petite and quite pretty, her limbs had since thickened and her face had grown heavy and coarse.

I imagine my mother, then eight or ten years old, standing with her sisters and brother on the packed dirt in front of their farmhouse. Near them, their parents wait. All of them wear their Sunday best, and the children have been forbidden to play until the visitor has arrived. Now the buggy, drawn by a single, copper-colored mare, a plume of brown dust lifting behind it, crests the hill and comes rocking down toward them.

The children draw back into the folds of their mother's great skirts as the buggy comes to a stop and the mysterious cousin steps down, wearing a long black dress, a broad-brimmed black hat, and a heavy black veil. My grandfather awkwardly extends a hand in greeting, fearful of what sort of hand may emerge from the woman's black dress to meet his. Now her hand is before her, before him, a slender and delicate hand gloved in black.

The woman sat in their slowly darkening parlor till nightfall, visiting about times and people lost and gone, and the children played in the dust until dark. Early in the evening she drove away, never to be seen by any of them again.

That story now in our imaginations, becoming a permanent part of us, my sister and I watch the violet shadows climb and eventually obscure the distant, hazy Wisconsin bluffs. We sit side by side on the porch swing, waiting to see what tale will be told next. We are learning the way in which stories end, how they drift into near silence, yet leave an after-ringing, like a bell.

༄ The cardplayers will expect refreshments at a midevening recess—sweet rolls, cake, coffee, tall bottles of grape and orange and strawberry soda brought over from the cooler at the station. My grandmother, who will serve these treats on pink and yellow Depression glass plates, moves deliberately about her kitchen, which is small and enameled yellow—like the inside of an egg—with little screened windows opening onto a patch of field corn that rustles and slaps in the breeze coming up the creek bed from the Mississippi each night. A white metal table, dewy with evening, stands under the windows, and on it, in a mason jar, is a yellow iris.

On a shelf next to the wood range sits a stained enameled pail, and there is the smell of mineral-rich water. It is my Uncle Elvy's job to fetch drinking water from the well behind the filling station. Waiting for the cardplayers to arrive, Elvy has grown impatient, so it is good that he has water to get. He lumbers off across the darkened side yard, swinging the pail. He loves pinochle, especially the part where you slam down your card and bang your knuckles on the table, but he also loves the sweet rolls and grape soda coming later. Besides his cerebral palsy, Elvy is diabetic and sometimes has seizures, but he craves sweet things. By feigning a weak spell he can usually manipulate his mother into giving him a roll or a few cookies, or permission to take a cold bottle of soda from the pop case.

Before the guests arrive, my grandfather goes through the pinochle ceremony, the pinochle blessing. He goes to a closet, takes out two card tables, and makes them yelp four times each as he jerks out their legs. Then he sets them down hard on the carpet on their black rubber hooves. From a cubbyhole in his disorderly desk he draws out two dog-eared decks of cards, carries them across the room as gingerly as if they were baited mouse-traps, and places them precisely at the center of the tables, pinpointing the spots where lightning could be expected to strike. Before the guests come, he furiously shuffles the cards as if to wring away any possibility of misfortune. His shuffling is like summer rain falling on leaves.

Though my grandfather is serious about cards, he is otherwise a fun-loving man. He can sometimes be persuaded to yodel or to jump his way through a brief jig in his shiny black Standard Oil shoes. When he was young he was considered a "sport," according to my grandmother. He had dark curls and courted her against her parents' wishes, parking his buggy on the road below her farm and stealing up through the woods to meet her in the shadows beside the house.

☙ He was born to Swiss immigrant parents on a farm on the Turkey River near Osterdock in 1874. The Turkey, which empties into the Mississippi about eight miles below my grandparents' house, was the traditional boundary between the Sioux on the north and the Sac and Fox to the south, and these tribes fought over access to the valley for many years. After the Sac and Fox and Sioux had been pushed out, the Winnebago, under the protection of the army, settled in the valley for a short time. Earlier, the shadowy Hopewell People lived there, hunting and fishing and building their burial mounds in the shapes of snakes and birds. My grandfather keeps in his cellar half a dozen five-pound sugar sacks full of arrow points and other stone tools he picked from the furrows behind his plow and from a low limestone shelf that runs along the river.

The Turkey valley was well worth fighting for. It is a place of steep hills, brooks that run white when it rains, and lush hardwood forests, interrupted by towering formations of yellow rock and tiny, sun-struck meadows. These little flats are misty with the kind of humidity that grows tall corn. Through these hills the Turkey runs wide and brown and glassy. It's a peaceful stream, but occasionally, swollen by spring rains, it rises out of its banks and carries away houses, livestock, barns, warehouses, and mill flumes. My grandfather tells us that in 1880, people in Osterdock paddled through the streets in boats and the railroad was washed out for miles. In 1902, my grandfather says, "everything imaginable" was swept away. Every few years there has been a devastating flood but, like horses run-ning back into a burning barn, the people in the valley go right back to their houses, shovel out the mud, and make coffee.

   ∽ Many years later, nostalgic in middle age for my

grandfather's stories, I will read that the mouth of the Turkey was the site of Iowa's only naval engagement of the Revolutionary War, an episode involving a flatboat with no more than a dozen terrified occupants aboard. Nobody got hurt. The British had captured Prairie du Chien and sent a company of men downriver to commandeer this little boat full of furs and supplies. They let the boatman go and used all the provisions, the tobacco and rum, to outfit a party of Canadians and Indians for an attack on St. Louis.

In 1805, Zebulon Pike camped opposite the mouth of the Turkey and, in 1820, Stephen W. Kearny paused there long enough to remark upon the "many pelicans, which at a distance make a very handsome shew."

In the 1830s, an Englishman, Charles Augustus Murray, went on a hunting expedition up the Turkey, but the Indians didn't appreciate the intrusion and drove off the game by shooting their guns in the air and setting the grass afire. In 1835, Albert Lea described the valley as "navigable about thirty miles, for any steam-boat on the Upper Mississippi. The finest soil, the finest timber, and the finest mines are to be found on this river of all that lie within the mining region. For agricultural purposes alone, it is highly desirable; but if the mineral wealth beneath the soil be considered, it is not wonderful that crowds of emigrants should be hastening to it, as they now are."

Those mines were lead mines but, now and then,

somebody would find a dime's worth of gold and set off quite a stir. It was not the mines that helped the emigrants to the Turkey valley prosper, but the rich black earth of the little meadows. My ancestors took that soil up into their hands and sniffed at it and crumbled it and planted corn and oats and wheat and garden vegetables. And irises.

~ The place where my grandfather was born and where he and my grandmother lived for forty years is about a dozen miles from the white bungalow by the Mississippi where they settled in their sixties. The year he was born, 1874, was the year barbed wire was invented. He will live ninety-eight years and will witness dozens of dazzling technological innovations—the telephone, electric lights, indoor plumbing, general anesthesia, gasoline-powered farm machinery, the automobile, radio, television, the atomic bomb, the Salk vaccine. He will live long enough to see, on his own flickering television set, men cavorting like boys in the lifting gray dust of the moon—yet he will never appear to be in any way surprised by what he reads in the *Dubuque Telegraph-Herald* or what he hears on the bone-colored Crosley radio that crackles from its shelf in the station. When at his post there, he sits back in his swivel chair behind the rolltop desk, puts his feet up on the desk, smokes his charred pipe, tips his cap to the engineers of passing freight trains—who wave and blow their whistles in greeting—and keeps up with the news with modest wonder and curiosity but never with awe.

He will be a Democrat all his life and will vote the straight ticket in thirteen presidential elections, walking miles overland to the polling place when the roads are impassable. He is tolerant of Republicans until they get evangelistic.

Salesmen frequently call on my grandfather, trying to sell him merchandise for his service station, and one summer day a carburetor cleaner salesman stops by. Though he does not intend to buy any carburetor cleaner, my grandfather has the courtesy to invite the man to stay for dinner. The salesman is a dignified old gentleman in suit pants and a white dress shirt stained yellow at the armpits. He dabs at his sweaty face with a handkerchief as they talk on the screened porch, waiting for my grandmother to put the meal on the table. I am sitting nearby, listening. When the carburetor cleaner salesman chances to say that Hoover hadn't been such a bad president after all, my grandfather stands, takes the man by the elbow, steers him to his car, and tells him never to set foot on his place again.

෴ My grandfather will have suffered enough death in his long life that by the end of his days he will be completely at ease with it and ready to let it gather him into its arms. He will outlive his parents, all of his brothers and sisters, his infant son, his wife, one of his daughters, and one son-in-law.

When he is in his mid-nineties, my mother and I will take him with us to the cemetery one Memorial Day. His wife and daughter are buried there, and my mother plans to plant some geraniums beside the family headstone. My grandfather is too stiff to get out of the car, and he sits in the backseat watching us attend to the graves. When we return to the car and are ready to drive away, an old man, one of the sextons at the cemetery, comes up and peers into the side window. "That you, John Moser?" he asks in a cracked voice.

"That's me, all right, Clarence," answers my grandfather.

"Well, how are you, John?"

"Well, Clarence, I'm ninety-four years old. I can't see too good, I can't hear too good, and I can't walk too good. You keep your shovel sharp!"

◠ I once asked my mother if she had any idea how her father could have lived so long, considering he was a lifelong pipe and cigar smoker and had a fondness for lard sandwiches on white bread. Without hesitation, she said, "Pickles. He loved pickles, and he ate them almost every day."

So it is pickles, a strong stomach for relentless change, and a remarkable constitution. He is to pay premiums on a health insurance policy for almost fifty years and never submit a claim. Late in his life, a doctor in Dubuque, studying an x-ray of his abdomen for what turns out to be a minor complaint, will inform my mother that her father has no appendix. It had probably burst when he was young, the doctor speculates, and somehow he lived through it.

∿ Lying in the grass beside the foundation of the white house is a broken headstone, a little bigger than a conventional brick, inscribed with the initials M.L.M. It is from the grave of Millard Laurel Moser, my grandparents' second child, who died in infancy. Somehow the stone got broken from its base and was brought down to the house, perhaps with the promise that someday it would be taken back to the cemetery and cemented into place. But it never got back. Years later, when my grandparents' house is sold, my mother will pick up the stone and take it to her house. Eventually I will take it home with me, where I will keep it on my writing desk. No one alive knows where Millard's grave is. On his small headstone is a dime-sized spot of white paint or whitewash, dropped there at some time when the house was repainted or when the stones along the driveway were whitewashed. The drop is the size of a doorbell, and sometimes I put my finger on it as if I thought it might open a door into the past.

∿ My grandfather is always to smell of warm motor oil and hot rubber tires and Prince Albert tobacco. He has the kind of strong, warm hands that a child can never forget, the kind that seem to hold sun in their skin and that know exactly what to do in any tearful emergency: how to fix a cap pistol when the hammer has fallen out with a heartbreaking clink, or how to pull a fishhook out of the ball of your thumb.

His Standard station is "full service" at a time when nobody has experienced service that is anything other than full. In mid-February, with a twenty-below-zero blizzard howling down the river, he'll wrap a scarf around his head, raise your old Chevy on the outdoor pneumatic hoist, take off a flat tire, patch it, and put it back on, all for a quarter. The purchase of a gallon of gas will get your tires and oil checked and your windows washed. He'll change your oil for the price of the oil.

The station is a gathering place for men who have nothing better to do than to sit in the shade and swap stories. Like my grandfather, these men are mostly old farmers retired from their fields. There is a pop case in which the bottles of soda—Nehi Grape, OhSo Orange, strawberry, cream soda—are submerged to their caps in water cooled by a block of ice. Between the station and the highway is an island of grass, and my grandfather has set up a horseshoe court there. Sometimes the men pitch horseshoes, their faces dark with concentration. Mostly they sit and talk. I want desperately to be a part of their company, to tell my own good stories, but it is impossible for a little boy to get a word in edgewise. So, with my Uncle Elvy, who can't be understood when he talks, I listen. Though I don't know it yet, I will one day be a writer, and my poems and stories will be my way of applying for acceptance into this same circle of old men, though they will all be ghosts by the time I am ready to tell them a story.

There are roadside filling stations like my grandfather's all over the country, often with some attraction to draw tourists in from the highway. Some of them have revolving cages in which trapped squirrels run forever. Others have glass museum cases displaying a few arrowheads.

The only special attraction at my grandfather's station is an old bachelor who lives in a shack on the wooded bluffs above the station. He has a talking fox terrier named Joel. Every day, weather permitting, the two of them come flying down the steep gravel road on a battered and rattling red bicycle. The dog bounces along in a wire basket fastened over the back tire, and the skinny old man, whose legs are long and whose knees stick out to either side, sits high astride a seat padded with a gunnysack.

The road is rough, and the bicycle leaps like a mountain sheep from ridge to ridge, rut to rut, clanging and ringing, crazy with broken spokes and loose fenders. The bachelor shouts to the dog as they come: "What's that you say there, Joel? What's that? You damn right, Dog! You goddamned right! You damn well better believe it!" Joel, his eyes wild with fear, gingerly turns and turns in his basket, borne through his life at breathtaking speed.

꩜ Forty years from now, while looking through a stack of old picture postcards I have purchased at a sale, I come upon one that I tack up over my desk. The picture is of a roadside filling station much like my grandfather's, and the card has been printed by one of the poorly aligned lithographic presses of the thirties. The photograph from which the lithographer worked lies like a ghost beneath the blurred coloring, and many of its details have been obscured: the trees that surround the building have no depth under the bright green wash; the souvenirs on display under the station's overhang run together in a splash of purple; and the face of the stationkeeper, as he stands proudly before his place of business, has been reduced to a drop of red.

The lithographer has gone to great pains to trace out, in bright yellow, the wording of the various signs nailed up here and there, so that some distant tourist, turning a creaking postcard rack in another filling station or roadside cafe, might be tempted to turn his station wagon full of small children toward this colorful haven of SOUVENIRS, COCA COLA, REST ROOM, NOVELTIES and TOWER.

It's this tower, rising a short distance out of the trees behind the station, that has again and again drawn my attention to this particular card. It's a wooden tower with a roofed platform. On one side of the railing that surrounds the floor hangs a big sign reading FREE TOWER. An open staircase leads up into the shadows under the roof.

Whatever lies beyond the green splotch of trees is unknown; there is nothing in the picture to tell me or my imaginary tourist whether the vista is of a sparkling lake or deep forest or sunlit river or sleeping giant. Certainly, whatever may be seen from this tower has not attracted a crowd. No one stands on the platform lifting a beckoning hand. There is no life in this scene but that of the man in his white shirt, standing beside the white wooden lawn chair (the kind whose seat is always wet from an overnight shower), with his expression obscured by that drop of red ink.

⤬ When the old men aren't around, I watch my grandfather throw pop bottle caps. When he was young, he played town-league baseball on teams like the Turkey River Gobblers, and as an old man he keeps his pitching arm limber by sailing pop bottle caps up over the top of the bluff across the road from the station. I will never be able to get the hang of it.

The Mosers are known for the way they thoroughly enjoy their lives, and my grandfather's niece once told me it used to be said that when the Mosers sang together after dinner, their voices filled the valley. He can remember and sing all the verses of "After the Ball was Over" and a half-dozen songs that nobody else can recall.

His father, Nick Moser, was born in a tiny village a few miles from Berne, Switzerland. He came to

America with his first wife, whose maiden name was Giesiger but whose first name has long been forgotten. They settled in New Philadelphia, Ohio, where my great-grandfather worked as a stonemason. According to my grandfather, old Nick built "many a cellar." In the 1850s, encouraged by a family friend from Switzerland who had settled in northeastern Iowa, they moved west, floating down the Ohio on a flatboat and then ascending the Mississippi. His wife's brother and his wife traveled west with them, settling in Dubuque.

Nick bought land in the Turkey River valley, near the tiny settlement of Osterdock, Iowa. I once asked my grandfather why his father had decided to settle on this rocky and hilly land that is so very difficult to farm, when it would have been easy to go another twenty miles west where the land levels out and offered black topsoil twenty feet deep. He told me they settled where they did, farming the little flats between the hills, because it reminded them of home.

By the time they got there, Clayton County was well established, the lands all claimed, the Indians gone. Nick and his first wife bought land from two men who were going on west. Then they settled in.

Nick's wife had two daughters by him before she died. His wife's brother also died at about that time, of the "cholery," as my grandfather said, and Nick then married Anna, the widow of his wife's brother, and brought her up from Dubuque. Anna already had five daughters, two by Mr. Giesiger and three from an earlier marriage in which she had also lost her husband, whose name had been Schroeder. In addition to the seven children already in the newlyweds' charge, Nick and Anna went on to have six sons and two daughters of their own. At ninety-six my grandfather, their youngest, frustrated at trying to remember the names of his fourteen older brothers, sisters, half brothers and half sisters, will describe his parents' family as a "real mix-up."

Nick developed some kind of disability early in their marriage—could it have been silicosis, "rock-dust sickness," from working with stone?—and my grandfather told me that the children and their mother had to do the farm work. And then he paused and added, somewhat sadly, "carelessly."

In a photograph of Nick and Anna, taken in old age on the front porch of their low-slung clapboard farmhouse, it's easy to see my grandfather's sunny features in his mother's round and smiling face. She is seated, enjoying the photographer's attention, much like her youngest son, who liked to have his picture taken, too. Lean old Nick, standing a few feet from her with his long white beard and suspenders, bites sourly on his pipe and angrily squints toward the camera.

From this photograph it is clear that theirs was a house made mostly for woman's work: the open porch, which runs the full length of the front, is fitted out with shiny cream cans, a washtub with wringers, and other domestic implements. There is a single rocking chair for Anna to use when her legs ached from hard work. A wooden churn stands in the shadow of the porch roof. The front yard is overgrown with weeds, and a sun-bleached board-walk on short stilts leads up to the house, a small stand of irises next to the walk.

∾ My grandfather and grandmother farmed the home place until they were in their sixties, raising three daughters and seeing them married and gone. Elvy was always to live with them.

My grandfather farmed with horses, spread their manure on his fields, weeded his crops with a hoe, harvested his corn by hand, and took his wheat to the mill in Osterdock. He kept a few hogs for meat, a few cows for milk, a couple of dozen chickens for eggs. My grandmother gardened and canned and preserved pork by frying it and packing it in lard. It was a system that didn't require much cash money. In the twenties, though, my grandfather bought his first automobile, which meant that he had to pay cash for gasoline. He tells me that as he paid for his first tank of gas he understood at once that the days of sustainable agriculture were over, that the wealth of his farmland would gradually drain away to the east.

∾ One cold late December day in the 1930s, Elvy, helping his mother with the housework, stuffed too many Christmas wrapping papers into the stove and the core of the brick chimney caught fire. The house burned to the ground while the three of them looked on. There were no rural fire departments in those days, and no fire insurance. When the flames played out, nothing was left but the little summer kitchen, which stood a few yards from the house.

They had known that they would one day have to sell the farm because they had no son who could farm it, since Elvy's cerebral palsy prevented him from doing any kind of physical work. They sold the land and the remaining farm buildings—a barn and a couple of sheds—to my grandfather's sister-in-law, Annie Moser, whose husband had died and whose sons were farming her ground and looking for more to work. Aunt Annie moved into the little one-room summer kitchen where she was to live for many years, sometimes accompanied by a cardboard box of baby chicks or a piglet she was nursing from a bottle. Next to the summer kitchen gaped the charred cellar hole, which over the years grew up in young cottonwood trees that in the autumn rattled their yellow leaves like flame.

My grandfather and grandmother rented a house in town while he built the Standard station and the little white house next to it. He was then in his sixties, and he was to operate the station for almost thirty years. After my grandmother died, he sold the business to a distant cousin and spent his days trying to keep busy around the house and yard. He and my uncle had a simple life. One Christmas in the late 1960s he will write me this letter:

> Dear Folks. We are well and hope you are too. We are eating Pancakes Soup and Meat Bread Pies and Pickled Apples Cookies some Cake and Ice Cream and are allright. Lester Moser was here Sunday night to visit us and stayed till 11 O Clock We Play Cards twice a week. It wont be long till Jack and Florence will come I dont know what day they will come I will have to get some Christmas Cards as I Probble will get some to. We have a trace of snow but Roads are good. I havent been out of the house the last two days will go uptown tomorrow to trade for food. I dont have much to write.
>
> John and Alva

~ In his early nineties he will get bored with sitting around the house and begin to pick up walnuts. He will set up a stump and folding chair in the cellar and sit down there for hours, cracking walnuts with a hammer, picking out the meats and putting them in cans. The word will get out that he has walnut meats to sell, and people will begin to appear. I ask him one day how the walnut business is going and he says that it is going almost too well. He can hardly keep up with the demand. "People just keep coming. Total strangers come right up to the door."

"How much do you charge?" I ask.

"I get a dollar for a three-pound coffee can full," he answers, proud to be making a profit and of having something useful to do. A dollar is plenty.

~ In my late fifties, I grow curious about the spelling of my Uncle Elvy's name—had he been christened Elvah, as the family Bible shows, or Alvah, as his gravestone reads, or Alva, as my grandfather spells it?—and, while on a daylong drive through that familiar country, I go to the county courthouse. I also want to look at the census records to see what life was like in the valley in the mid-1800s.

The courthouse stands in its leafy square, its great gray bulk afloat on the deep and slowly rolling ocean of time. It is a kind of buoy, marking a submerged reef of obscure laws, its tower like a silent bell. It is November, and the towering maples that surround the building have lost nearly all of their leaves except for a few unsettled lawsuits pinned here and there.

The courthouse marks a point on the globe at which all of the forces of life crowd in and rub together, blue wool upon gray wool, heating the upper rooms so that as I glance up from the sidewalk a young woman throws up a rattly window sash and leans out, licking her lips in the delicious candy of cold air. She is wearing a crisp-looking white blouse and has a red scarf tied at her neck. She makes a lovely flag, with far more life to her than sour Old Glory, sternly snapping its fingers high above.

The oak door at the entrance weighs a hundred pounds and swings on brass hinges a quarter of an inch thick. One does not draw open such portals with a frivolous heart. Beyond the entrance, marble stairs ascend into the lofty mahogany-paneled chambers. There is a weariness about these steps, like people burdened by a sense of history.

In a room on the third floor are shelves of bound ledgers, and a helpful young woman tells me how I can find what I'm looking for. The records for the year in which my Uncle Elvy was born, 1905, have been lost, a mystery. All of the ledger pages are there, numbered in sequence, but there are no entries for 1905.

Next I look at the 1856 census. There were, officially:

> 2,696 Dwelling Houses
> 2,884 Families
> 8,227 Males
> 6,960 Females
> 6 Colored Persons
> 15,187 Total Males and Females
> 5,531 Married
> 334 Widowed
> 1,958 Native Voters
> 875 Naturalized Voters
> 913 Aliens
> 2,555 Militia
> 11 Deaf and Dumb
> 3 Blind

1 Insane

6 Idiotic

2,097 Owners of Land

5 Paupers

Those six "Colored Persons" didn't count in the total number of males and females. I know from other reading that one of those five paupers (or perhaps one of the six colored persons) would have been Rebecca "Aunt Becky" Clues, a mulatto who, according to the county history, had been the slave of Governor Clarke of Missouri but who had been freed by him after she had miraculously turned white following an attack of bilious fever. She came north and, after working as a cook and housekeeper for many years, became a ward of the county.

The census also suggests a good deal about how people spent their days:

$18,120 Domestic Manufactures

$40,787 General Manufactures

50,020 Acres improved Land

211,324 Acres unimproved Land

3,218 Acres Meadow

7,192 Tons Hay

260 Bushels Grass Seed

14,392 Acres Spring Wheat:

   252,835 Bushels Harvested

470 Acres Winter Wheat:

   5,603 Bushels Harvested

4,505 Acres Oats: 170,842 Bushels Harvested

12,112 Acres Corn: 507,579 Bushels Harvested
689 Acres Potatoes: 78,237 Bushels Harvested
5,603 Hogs sold for $46,030
1,980 Cattle sold for $71,123
165,261 Lbs. Butter made,
15,272 Lbs. Cheese made
10,669 Lbs. Wool raised.

∽ On that summer evening in 1949, when I am ten, Annie Moser, the sister-in-law who bought my grandfather's home place, and her bachelor son, Clarence, are coming to play pinochle. Aunt Annie is a delightful old woman, full of fun. Tonight she is wearing a navy blue go-to-meeting dress. She likes children more than she likes pinochle, and she will spend a good part of the evening playing with Judy and me. When they arrive, she will bring a half pint of coffee cream, separated in an old Duval separator that looks like an oversized drinking fountain.

My sister and I will beg her to sing an old song we like:

> Twenty froggies went to school
> Down beside the rushing pool.
> "We must be in time," said they,
> "First we study, then we play.
> That is how we keep the rule
> As we froggies go to school."
> Master bullfrog, grave and stern,
> Calls the classes in their turn,
> Tells them how to say "Ker-chog,"

> *and to leap from log to log.*
> *Twenty little coats so green,*
> *Twenty vests so neat and clean.*
> *"We must be in time," says they,*
> *"First we study, then we play.*
> *That is how we keep the rule*
> *As we froggies go to school."*

Completing the song, she will cackle like a hen on a nest. The laughter is worth more than the song, than almost any song. Fifty years later I will still be able to hear it.

Clarence looks like the Mosers—like my grandfather, like my Uncle Elvy—with a round bald head and a toothy smile. While we are waiting for the other players I ask him to tell us the story of their visit to Omaha. I have heard it before, but in our family we tell our stories over and over. He speaks with just a touch of German in his voice.

Early one spring he and Aunt Annie had decided to drive to Omaha to visit my mother's older sister, Florence, and her husband, my Uncle Jack Mayo, a four-hundred-mile trip. When they got there they were unable to find a Jack Mayo in the phone directory. Jack's given name was Ralph and, though they looked under Mayo, they didn't think to look under Ralph Mayo. Too thrifty to stay in a motel, they drove around for a long time, asking people if they knew Jack Mayo. Then, as it was getting dark, they decided to sleep in their car. They found a lot

32

down by the Missouri River where construction equipment was being parked, and they drove in between two of the machines and settled in for the night. Chuckling and dabbing at his eyes, Clarence tells how they slept one to the front seat and one to the back, a good-sized seventy-year-old woman and her two-hundred-pound son, and how cold it was, and how all night long huge watchdogs would stand with their paws against the windows, snarling.

⟋ Also coming to play cards are Elmer and Lizzie Morarend, my grandmother's brother's son and his round, shy wife who speaks with a pronounced German accent. She often finishes her sentences with "already," as in, "Have you finished your canning yet a'ready?" Lizzie's ancient, mysterious father, known to us as Grosvater, is to come with them. He speaks only a little English and never takes his hat off.

Lizzie wears her hair in tight ringlets that she makes with an old-fashioned stove-heated curling iron. When she puts her folded hands on her lap, the flesh on her wrists looks creased to the bone, as if her hands were hinged like those of a doll. And, like a doll, her head rolls when she talks.

She has high blood pressure and tries every new pill that comes out. She has so many prescriptions that she stands the bottles in a line on the kitchen windowsill and moves from left to right each morning, taking a pill from each. New prescriptions and refills are added to the right, empty bottles at the far left go in the trash.

Elmer is like all of the Morarends: tall, thin, and shy. In Elmer the essence of that family shyness had been distilled to a pure, sweet concentrate. He has a tiny voice, squeaky as a hinge, and he keeps his long hands folded together at his waist so they cannot fly out and fasten on some kind of trouble. He holds his face well down out of the light of conversation, and what he knows of the world he's learned by peering out from under his thin eyebrows.

He is my Uncle Elvy's sometime fishing partner, and Elvy will be glad to see him. He drives a black 1949 Chevrolet two-door, never exceeding twenty miles per hour, and he sometimes drives Elvy on down the river to sloughs beyond the reach of his walks. Often there is a cane pole extending from the back window on the passenger's side, a bobber rattling against it, and he keeps a fishy-smelling gunnysack in the trunk.

The older Morarends, Elmer's and my mother's grandparents, came from Mecklenberg, in Germany. In my grandmother's house is a photograph of my great-grandfather, John Dietrich Morarend, standing in the center aisle of a general store in a wide-brimmed black hat and a long black coat. He and several clerks are looking toward the camera, but I can't read much in his face with its long white beard. He looks like a German Protestant zealot. There is also a small photo of his wife, Dorothea, posed round-shouldered on a chair in a clearing in the woods and glaring into the camera. I know they had thirteen children, losing four boys as infants.

∾ Years from now, when my mother is an old woman, we will visit the pioneer rock church that my great-grandfather Morarend helped build in the 1850s. Vandals have broken the lock on the door, and have stolen the pewter communion cup from its place on the altar. They have torn the brackets for the oil lamps away from the walls, leaving black wounds like bullet holes. Over the fifty years since regular services were discontinued, the church has been attacked again and again.

Mr. and Mrs. Reimann, of the local cemetery association, have opened the new lock and invited us to enter—my mother; my mother's best friend, Ruth Kregel; my wife; my son; and I. This church is one of the few ties I have to my great-grandfather, and I fasten on every detail as if it were a button on his coat.

The building is cool and slightly damp, like the shadowy bluffs nearby from which the yellow blocks of stone were quarried. The walls are thick, encasing our hushed voices. The wooden floorboards knock under our feet.

There's a big wood stove in the middle of the room. The pews are simple, made of pine and paint-ed white. On the north wall, the pulpit stands on a raised platform with steps leading up to it. Over it is an octagonal shade, draped with purple fabric, a German Lutheran purple, the deep purple of some varieties of iris.

As we stand at the front of the church, listening to Mrs. Reimann tell us some of the history, my mother sits in one of the pews by a window and folds her hands over her purse in the way her mother folded hers. Mother is in her seventies now, and listening not to what is being said but to words deep inside her. Mrs. Reimann's words float all about her like falling leaves, while her mind reaches into the distant past. The past shows on her face as a faint youthful smile. She is a widow now and wears her loss with grace. My father has been dead for five years. Light falls through the window and across her shoulders and flares in her neatly groomed hair.

On a wall nearby, two framed portraits glower down upon us. They are those of the first minister and his wife, fierce-looking people, the minister's jaw clenched tightly. Great-grandfather Morarend would have known these people well. The Reimanns tell us that the minister and his wife had six children, and that the family lived in the two small rooms over our heads. They invite us to follow and we climb the creaking stairs.

A light frost of dust covers the floors in the minister's rooms, covers the deep sills of the windows. Our voices echo. In one corner a small iron stove has taken on the pastor's dark, sulking personality. Near the ceiling in one of the rooms, stenciled in a darker green than the paint on the walls, is a simple repeated fleur-de-lis in pale lavender (based on the iris?), something to stand throughout the next hundred years against the starkness of that churchly life—surely the work of an infinitely patient feminine hand.

～ Among the many children on the Morarend side of the family is Aunt Laura, my grandmother's sister. She and her husband, Pete Noack, are too shy and reclusive to come for pinochle, but my grandfather says that their son, Harvey, and his wife, Helen, may stop by for coffee later.

Among the family photographs in my grandparents' house is a studio portrait taken early in this century. Three young men and two boys are posed with musical instruments. To the right, standing behind a harp, is my great-uncle Pete. Next to him, also standing, are his two sons, Harold and Harvey, the first cradling a violin to his breast, the second holding a flute before him like a candlestick. The other two men in the picture are about the same age as my great-uncle. One of them sits holding a trumpet on one knee, and the other behind a small set of drums. The man behind the drums was a neighbor of the Noacks, Pete Kickbush. I do not know who the trumpet player was.

The picture was taken in front of a floral backdrop in a little studio above the harness shop in Guttenberg, Iowa, sometime just before World War I. The handsome yet sad-looking boy with the violin will die as a very young man, a victim of the same crippling inflammatory arthritis that years later will disable his brother. Their father will wear the same quiet smile throughout his long life, while his golden harp gathers light to itself in a corner of his parlor.

~ Years from this pinochle evening, looking at the picture of these musicians, I am reminded that there was a time when music had to be sought out like honey in a hollow tree. There was no radio as we know it, with hundreds of stations playing music twenty-four hours a day. If you wanted music you either made it yourself or hitched up the horses to the farm wagon or buggy and drove to a place where you might find it. My great-uncle's chamber group, assembling in whichever farmhouse might invite them, drew families from miles around. Music was worth more then.

When I was a boy, Uncle Pete was already an old man and had given up the harp. Harvey and his wife, Helen, shared the house with Uncle Pete and Aunt Laura. Harvey and Helen slept in the room where he had slept with Harold as a boy.

We visited them once or twice each summer. As we drove into the lane, the four of them would slowly materialize, each from a different corner of their small acreage. Uncle Pete, rawboned, rosy cheeked, chewing tobacco, would appear at the edge of the apple orchard, wearing bib overalls and a straw hat. Helen would come up from the vegetable garden, wearing an old housedress and running a hand back through her iron-colored hair. Harvey, stooped and twisted to one side by his disease, would come around the side of the house, steadying himself with one hand on the clapboards. Last, and very slowly, thin and shy Great-Aunt Laura would emerge from the kitchen door, having taken a moment to wrap herself in a gray wool shawl, although it was midsummer and so hot that their dog barked at us without crawling out from under the porch.

Their acreage was set into the edge of the timber along the high ridge that divides the good flat farmland of eastern Iowa from the tumbling, rocky woodland of the Mississippi valley. While most of my mother's family had settled among the trees and rocks below, a few of them had pushed on up to the top, where the rich flatlands drifted without interruption into the west. It was to the west that their house faced, so that in late afternoon when Uncle Pete sat in his caned rocker on the front porch, spitting tobacco juice into the bridal wreath, the sun sat red on his lean and peaceful face.

He'd given up formal work years before. He'd once been the county assessor and had held other jobs from time to time, but when I knew him his family lived on the vegetables from their well-tended garden, the meat and eggs from their chickens and ducks, and what little money they got by selling apples from the gnarled old trees and rich honey from their fragrant blossoms. They had no electricity, no running water. Aunt Laura baked bread nearly every day, and on those days she didn't, she mended and cleaned and washed clothing and canned.

They'd invite us into the house and offer us freshly baked bread with butter and sorghum molasses or honey. We'd sit in the parlor and visit, Uncle Pete's harp impressive in its corner and Harvey's flute gathering dust on the top of a glass-fronted bookcase. The Noacks were quiet people, and our conversation would be filled with long, awkward pauses while all of us jiggled our coffee cups in their saucers and traced the geometric pattern in the linoleum with our downturned eyes.

Sometimes we'd take Aunt Laura for a ride down to the general merchandise store in Osterdock, one of the last remaining buildings in a little pioneer settlement on the Turkey River. It was a mile's drive, straight downhill. We'd have to roll the windows up tight, because Aunt Laura was prone to take a chill, though the rest of us could scarcely breathe for the heat. When the car started to roll downhill, gaining speed, Aunt Laura, from within the folds of her shawl, would make a long, soft cooing sound, like a pigeon on its roost.

The store sold big ice cream cones, a treat for my sister and me. As we stood eating them beside the car, Aunt Laura and my grandmother, sisters who looked so much alike they could have been twins, both dressed in the cool colors of summer shadows, drew apart from us and quietly visited, looking at each other as if each were watching herself in a full-length mirror, a little embarrassed by what she saw. There was a quiet peace between my grandmother's brothers and sisters, and they must have had a wonderful childhood together on the old Morarend place, which lay nearby.

Then it was back up to the house and a lengthy farewell between the two sisters under the shade trees. As we drove away, the four of them would move back into whichever corner he or she might have materialized from, there to wait, it seemed to me, until we came again.

~ When Harvey was a young man, playing the flute in the family chamber group, he was "discovered" by a professor of music from the University of Iowa. How this professor could have wandered out into rural Clayton County and found him is a mystery to me, but Harvey was given a scholarship to the university, and when he finished his music degree he was asked to stay and teach. After a few years he went on to become a concert musician, and he played in many of the great orchestras of his day, both in the states and in Europe. At some point, on one of his rare visits home, he married Helen and took her back on the road with him.

Their life must have been happy and exciting. Later, when I knew them, neither spoke of those days. As Harvey neared middle age, the crippling family disease began to affect him. His hands grew stiff and twisted, and his spine curved forward. He played as long as he was able to, and then the two of them returned to the home place. There they lived out their days, surviving Pete and Laura by a number of years.

The last time I saw Harvey alive was at my grandmother's funeral. He was by then so badly stooped that as he sat in a folding chair in the church basement during the after-services luncheon, I had to sit on the floor at his feet to visit with him. Still, he was quiet and friendly, uncomplaining, a farm boy from Clayton County who'd traveled all over Europe and didn't show a trace of it. Helen was by his side, grown grayer and more distracted by worry, but pleasant.

When Harvey died, I attended his funeral, and after the graveside services, the neighbors who had known him all his life remarked upon what an odd child he'd been, how much alone and set apart he'd always seemed. He could have been a good farmer, one of them said, or a storekeeper, or a miller, but off he went with his flute, gallivanting all over the world, a Noack like his father, never wanting to work too hard or too long. Look what it all came to: nothing, they said—a wife left with no money, a drafty old house with no lights or water or so much as a radio to play in the evenings for company, a few old sticks of furniture, an old harp split like a gourd from dryness, and a flute full of dust.

⌒ Such music there is in the past.

Clarence and Parthenia Meyer are also stopping by for coffee later. Parthenia is one of my mother's favorite cousins and the only daughter of my Great-aunt Annie and Uncle Fred Moser. The two girls grew up on adjacent farms and often played together as little girls. Parthenia is a big woman, a Moser through and through, with a broad smile of fine teeth and a wen on the side of her nose. Years from now, when Parthenia is in her seventies, she will tell me about her late husband's polka band, the Jolly Ridge Hillbillies. She said she bought his first accordion for him, as a gift, when they were "sparking" back in 1931. The accordion was an El Italia model, and had a bright red bellows covered with white polka dots.

One day, as a surprise for her, he brought the accordion to the country school where she was teaching and played it for her pupils. One little boy went home that evening and told his parents, "Teacher's feller came to school and played music for us on a thing all fastened together with red neckties!"

Clarence married Parthenia and went on to play music all his life. He farmed for a living, and in the evenings, after the hard work of the long day had been set aside, he and his three sons, each of whom he'd taught to play various instruments, filled their big frame house with music. I remember it from my childhood as being like a huge box of light and laughter and music. At Saturday night dances,

Clarence and his friends, squeezing out waltzes and polkas and schottisches, kept generations of my plump German cousins gasping for breath and sweating through the backs of their best dresses and overalls.

∾ My sister and I are already tired, and the pinochle players have not even started their game. I have worn myself out swinging from the tree and digging fishworms and running around in the yard and sitting at the filling station listening to the old men talk and laugh. I also feel small and insignificant and set aside among the cardplayers, who are more serious about cards than small boys are likely to be.

As they sit down to play and the clip-clip-clip of the deal goes round, I go out onto the screened porch, where a cool breeze blows off the Mississippi now hidden out there in the darkness. At the end of the porch, a thick-stemmed tulip vine climbs over the screen and in the thin light I see a patch of white among the leaves. I move close and see that it is the belly of a field mouse who has gone to sleep under a leaf. He sleeps so soundly that he does not know I am there. I carefully touch the fur that extends through the screening and for an instant he doesn't move. Then he awakens and scampers away.

On the seat of the porch swing are a couple of old rag rugs, and I first sit there, then lie down. The crickets are loud in the grass and the frogs boom from the river bottom. On the breeze is the smell of the river and, from close at hand, the fragrance of iris. Soon I have fallen asleep and will not awaken till the players are leaving, near midnight, and my mother comes for me. When I awaken I will have the woven pattern of a rag rug impressed in my cheek.

When we are staying there, Elvy gives up his room to me. It is small and cool and blue and damp from the river bottom air. I sleep in his big soft saggy bed. My mother and my sister sleep in my grandparents' bed, and Grandma and Grandpa sleep on a fold-out couch in the living room. As I go to sleep again I can hear the squeak of the fold-out couch being opened. My grandmother has made up the daybed in the dining room for Elvy. He curls on his side because he has trouble breathing when on his back, and she has covered him with a yellow blanket.

∾ My grandmother was buried on the nineteenth of January, 1962. At dawn that morning, a newsman at the radio station at La Crosse announced that it was twenty-two below. Through the night, a gusty wind from the northwest had buffeted my grandparents' house, and as I lay in my Uncle Elvy's bed heaped with comforters I could see the lace curtains billowing away from the frost-covered window as they filled with the sharp, shallow breath of the cold.

My uncle had spent the night on the sofa bed, and

I knew that it must have been he who had turned on the weather report at so early an hour. For many years my grandmother had begun her day by listening with him to the first morning news, and, like the rest of us who felt her loss, my uncle had begun to grasp for threads of continuity, however feeble these might have been.

His bed sagged in the middle with the ghost of his bulk. I had fought the invitation of that hollow throughout those long hours in which I had lain awake. But at the sound of the radio I awoke to find myself nestled in the mold of my uncle's body, looking up at the cracked ceiling as it emerged in the gathering light. I got out of bed and dressed quickly in the cold.

My grandfather and uncle were sitting at the dining room table when I came into the room. The curtains were open at the window, and beyond the frosty glass the landscape was gray and black. The sofa bed had been made up and folded away. Grandfather had already dressed for the funeral, which wasn't until eleven o'clock. He wore a gray wool suit whose coat was too tight across his belly to be buttoned, a light blue shirt, and a dark red tie. On the table before him sat his good felt hat. He was looking out the window toward the cemetery, which lay on the hillside a few hundred yards behind the house.

On the day before, two men hired by the mortuary had gone to the cemetery early to prepare the grave. They had lined up four fifty-gallon steel drums on the site and had built fires in them. It was past noon before the heat had thawed the earth enough for their picks, and they had spent the morning sitting in their idling pickup, occasionally getting out to take scrap lumber from the back and toss it in the barrels.

The smoke could be seen from the house, and my grandfather had spent the afternoon at the table, his hands around an empty coffee cup, watching the white columns rise through the cold, clear air.

༄ After a service at the church, we followed the hearse to the cemetery, where the snow was more than a foot deep and capped with a crust of ice through which the pallbearers broke their way. My uncle followed, my father supporting him. Once he lunged forward to touch a corner of the casket, stumbled, and fell to one knee. My father helped him to his feet and he stood dabbing at his swollen eyes with red fists covered with snow.

The green tent flapped in the fierce cold, and we huddled together while the minister read from his book, raising his voice above the whine of the wind. During the final prayer, a gust scattered flowers among our feet and blew them away over the snow.

Behind us, the black oaks climbed the steep bluffs. Before us, the brushy hillside slid away to the bottomland, where the roof of my grandparents' house, the filling station, and my grandmother's chicken house showed through the bare trees in the yard. I could see that a light had been left on in her kitchen as if someone were waiting for us there.

~ Then my grandfather was gone.

A few years after his death, his nephew, Ira Friedlein, shows me an old photograph of a family reunion, my great-grandparents' family, sixty happy Mosers gathered in front of a farmhouse that has been gone for half a century. The picture, which is the color of a tea stain on a lace tablecloth, is framed in gilded plaster. It hangs on the living room wall of Ira's house, next to the color photographs of his children and grandchildren.

During the past year Ira has lost his wife, and he lives alone in their house at the edge of town. He stands close to me, enthusiastically pointing out the people in the photograph with the tip of his finger. It's an old, farmer's finger, tanned and wrinkled, with a thick nail, carefully pared, most probably with a pocketknife. He's a short man, like my grandfather. I can look down upon his bald head, which is white from years of wearing hats. In his face, reflected in the glass over the photograph, I see my grandfather's face and the faces of the other Mosers I have known.

He tells me that there were once three John Mosers in the county when he was a boy: Long John, a distant cousin; Short John, my grandfather; and Skip

Level Johnny, another distant cousin who got his nickname by being shorter than the one and taller than the other. Chuckling, Ira tells me that Skip Level Johnny, a lifelong bachelor, used to walk all over the countryside, dropping in on neighbors just as they sat down to supper. "My," he'd say, "conversation always goes better when you sit up to a table!"

Ira is seventy-nine years old. He tells me that of all the sixty people in the photograph, only he and my Aunt Mabel are still alive. The picture was taken before my mother was born. He puts the tip of his finger under Mabel's chin, a tiny baby on my grandmother's lap, then under his own chin, the chin of a baby crooked in his father's arm. In the picture, Baby Ira looks up at the sky, perhaps following some sparkling mote or shining filament of spider web.

∾ On the radiator by the window in my Uncle Elvy's room at the nursing home, my father has placed a glass vase with three blue irises. They have traveled far in the more than seventy years since they stood outside the house where my uncle was born.

Near the end of his life, Elvy sits in a straight chair, looking like an old wooden rain barrel caved in upon itself. His wet chin rests on his breastbone and his arms hang down on either side of his chair. He breathes very softly, his chest scarcely lifting. He has lost thirty pounds since his father died. Within a few months, he too will die.

His room's large windows are curtained with a filmy blue material through which he can look across the lawn and past the highway into a shimmering field of corn. In similar rooms all up and down the hallway, other old men are looking out at the corn. The bed in which my grandfather slept each night and in which he died is neatly made up and pushed against the opposite wall.

My mother kneels before him, paring his toenails with a clipper that cuts with a hard snap. Every week she and my father come to visit, driving seventy-five miles. Just as she did when her father was living, she takes the laundry home with her and brings it back the following week. She cuts and combs her brother's hair, she clips his nails. Her own hair is lightly rinsed with blue and her Merle Norman makeup has been meticulously applied. She wears a businesslike blue suit of her own making.

My father has hurriedly left the room and he now strides briskly along a gleaming hallway where old people in wheelchairs call to him and reach to touch him as he passes. Though he is by nature a sociable man, his face is tight and white and he looks straight ahead, not acknowledging their pleas. They are not hurt by his behavior. All day the dead have been walking back and forth among them, pretending not to know their names. Names, dates, places—the old people are lost in a shifting confusion of detail:

an enameled water dipper swings from a nail, making a black arc on the wallpaper behind it; a pillow in a case embroidered with daisies falls to the floor between a bed and a wall.

A moment ago, on the mirror above the sink in my uncle's small bathroom, there appeared a sign. Foolishness, of course, to see a sign, but there it was. On the glass, where perhaps my uncle had at some time steadied himself in a moment of dizziness, there was a full handprint. The handprint fell across my father's face when he looked at himself. Suddenly death was all about him, like the air itself. The cold steel handrails clung to the tiled walls, their flanges like the mouths of leeches. Condensation from the cold toilet tank dripped onto the floor, corroding the bolts on the base of the stool. The fluorescent light buzzed like a fly.

Now, as he rushes through people calling and calling to him, his heart tapping in his ears, he feels how frail and light he may soon become. He wants more gravity, he wants to hold himself down, to keep himself together for a little longer, to cherish the softening muscles wrapped like weights around his bones. How little his skull of thin, translucent bone must weigh. How fragile and infirm (and yet how precious to him) are its tiny sutures, the pearly, polished sockets for the eyes.

He stares past the girl painting her nails at the information desk, past the big windows in the visiting room that open upon beds of white petunias

51

drooping in the heat, past the empty iron benches in the neatly mown grass. The cornfield looks as if it were made of electricity. It has suddenly come upon him that he is seventy years old and incapable of walking in any other direction than straight into the future. Flowered sport shirt; thin, spotted arms.

∿ My father died the following New Year's Eve.

More and more frequently since I entered my fifties I have begun to see his hands out at the ends of my arms. Just now, the left and more awkward hand lies curled in my lap while the right one massages the beard on my chin. On the ring finger of the left is the silver wedding band that my wife gave me, not my father's gold ring with its little yellow sapphire. But I am not deceived; this wearing of my ring on his ring finger is part of my father's respectful accommodation to me and of my life and marriage. Mine have succeeded his, which is, as he would have said, only as it should be.

I recognize his hands despite the ring. They are exactly as I remember them from his middle age— wrinkled, of course, with a slight sheen to the tiny tilework of the skin, with knotted, branching veins, and with thin dark hair that sets out from beneath the shirtcuffs as if to cover the hand but that within an inch thins and disappears as if there were a kind of glacial timberline there. There is, as we know, a field of coldness just beyond the reaching tips of our fingers; this hair has been discouraged and has fallen back.

As a young man my father had been a drapery salesman in a department store, and ever after his hands were at their best when smoothing fabric for display—the left one holding a piece of cloth unrolled from a bolt while the right lovingly eased and teased the wrinkles from it, his fingers spread and their tips lightly touching the cloth as if under them was something grand and alive like the flank of a horse. I can feel the little swirls of brocade beneath the ball of his thumb.

These hands have never done hard physical work, but they are not plump, or soft, or damp, or cool. Nor are their nails too carefully clipped or too carefully buffed and polished. They are firm, solid, masculine hands, and other men feel good about shaking them. They have a kind of brotherly warmth, and when they pinch the selvage of the drapery fabric and work it just a little between thumb and finger, they do it with power and confidence. There are pairs of hands like these—some brown, some black, some white—in every bazaar in the world—hands easing and smoothing, hands flying like doves through the dappled light under time-riddled canvas.

I would like to be held by these hands, held by them as they were when I was a child and I seemed to fall within them wherever I might turn. I would like to feel them warm and broad against my back and would like to be pressed to the breast of this man with a faint perfume of aftershave, tiny brown moles on his neck, and a necktie whose knot is slightly darkened by perspiration. Now he has taken his glasses off and set them on the mantel and there are small red ovals on the sides of his nose. I reach to touch them and find them wet, as if I were touching something deep inside him. Now I hear him singing, softly singing, the words buzzing deep in his chest.

But these old hands of his are past all that. They lie side by side in my lap, their palms turned up as if to catch this fleeting moment as it falls away. But as I peer down into them they begin to move on their own, to turn and shift. I watch the left hand slowly rise to place its palm against my heart, and watch the right rise swiftly to enfold the other.

～ Elvy's death follows my father's by just a few months.

On the day of his funeral I am four hundred miles away, but I am with him all day, as if in a waking dream.

At the funeral home his body looks smaller, lighter—light as a dry leaf about to be shifted a little, about to tick and skitter along a road and then flutter away on the wind.

The only thing about him that looks natural this morning as he lies in his casket are his big wrinkled hands, fanned together across his shirt front. For an instant I imagine they hide a good pinochle hand from Lizzie Morarend who, with her laughing, dancing eyes, sometimes tried to sneak a look. After the last fumbling shuffle and the last slow deal around, my Uncle Elvy has dealt himself a pinochle—the jack of diamonds and the queen of spades—and is pressing the cards close to his silenced heart.

The Mueller Funeral Home sits on a side street two blocks from the river. All over the Midwest it has been snowing off and on for two days—the fine, dusty, sidewise-flying, needle-tipped snow of early February—and a furious cold whistles down the street and out across the frozen Mississippi. My uncle's memorial service is scheduled to begin in a half hour, but so far no one has arrived. Bouquets of cut flowers bank the gray metal casket, their fragrance draped over the air. On a walnut stand the visitation book has been scratched with a dozen signatures.

The Mueller Funeral Home is the one white house that's always freshly painted, the only house within fifty miles with curtains in the basement windows—pink ones that hide the embalming lab. Franklin Mueller, the proprietor, is at this moment in his office behind a heavy white door, typing an official document that has to do with my uncle's death. Elvah Bert Moser led a life almost altogether deprived of official documentation, and the time has come to complete his meager file. What would we find in that thin manila folder? A birth certificate dated 1905; his Social Security disability application papers; the certificate of death from complications following surgery; and, finally, an itemized statement from Mueller "for services rendered."

In that folder there ought to be a lock of Elvy's

beloved mother's hair, a fishhook threaded with the dry brown beads of a long dead worm, a few caramel wrappers, an iron throwing shoe, and a yellowing prescription in old Doctor Palmer's trembling hand: *Sodium dilantin, take one each day for spells.*

I stand in the warm carpeted entryway, hoping that Mueller will not hear me and come out to catch my hand in both of his as if it were a butterfly. I want to stand here quietly, looking out through the etched glass windows of the double doors to see who may come up the sidewalk through the falling snow. Surely they will all come, by and by, the ghosts of those who have gone before.

Facing the casket are rows of empty folding chairs, set out in neat arcs like ripples spreading on the surface of a pond. From small speakers painted the ivory enamel of the woodwork, recorded organ music drones: Buxtehude, Handel. The paper on the walls, white peonies on a rose-colored field (how I wish that they were irises), is the sort of thing one might expect to find in a formal dining room. Surely this was once such a room, when the funeral home was really a home, with Schubert or Haydn tinkling from a windup music box on the sideboard and the beveled glass of the leaded windows sprinkling rainbows over fine linen and Haviland china.

In the entryway are a few plush chairs, so new they look otherworldly, their rich upholstery unworn, their varnished arms unscratched. There's a yellow oak lectern upon which is set a guest book that smells of ink and glue. The beige cover is slightly tacky to the touch. A few names, all familiar to me—Meyer, Friedlein, Stickfort, Kuempel, Kann—record the visits paid to the body during the viewing period by families that have been in this valley for nearly a hundred years.

Now, through the framework of leafy vines etched into the glass, I see them coming—parking their prewar Chevrolets and Fords and Plymouths along the street and stepping toward me through snowdrifts, the men's hair combed in wisps across their balding heads, their heavy wives with flowered headscarves knotted under double chins, all of them in winter coats pulled close around shoulders whitening with snow.

ᴥ But for now, it is summer, 1949, and I am still a little boy. Our time with our grandparents is over. My father has come to drive us home. Before we leave, he fills his arms with tiger lilies picked beside the house, and we start out walking up the gravel road to the cemetery. It is now too late for irises. They have shriveled to rags. My sister and I walk on either side of him. I look back and see my grandmother stooped in her garden, picking a few vegetables for us to take home. My uncle shuffles across the yard toward the filling station.

There's a granite monument topped with the carved figure of a seated girl. Her head is bowed, and she looks sadly into her empty arms, which are pitted from many years of rain and snow. In the hollow of those arms my father arranges the bright orange flowers and steps back. We do not know whose grave this is, whose loss the statue memorializes. My father's eyes mist over, for he is a soft-hearted man, easily moved. His is a very special sort of foolishness, and my sister and I are learning it from him. We carry flowers to this girl at the close of each summer. It's what my father calls "tradition."

∼ An April morning, nearly fifty years later. My mother has recently died, at age eighty-nine, my last living link to the stories of her family. She has left me to reckon with a rapidly fading past that will, from the day of her death forward, be, as Edwin Muir described it, little more than a confusion of lights on a ground of darkness.

This is the rainy season, when the Turkey River bears close watching. In Osterdock an old man in a cap with earflaps leans over the bridge rail to observe the water inching up the supporting columns. He has a red face and a drop of clear moisture at the end of his nose. It's a new bridge, made of concrete, wide and solid. The former bridge was narrow, riveted together out of steel, and it shuddered ominously whenever a floating tree trunk bumped a support. Nearby is the broken and overgrown foundation of the general merchandise store where we once bought ice cream cones, where my grandmother and her sister, Laura, waited outside in the shade of a tree. The old man tells me he cannot remember my mother, Vera Moser, or her brother, Elvy, or her parents, John and Liz, but he says with a smile that the hills along the Turkey River are full of Mosers and Morarends.

Four hundred miles from this new bridge that reaches not merely over a flooded river but pushes forward out of the past, the irises in my garden will soon bloom. Their petals are tightly furled, spun into tight little cones of rich color, yellow and blue. Within a day or two they will be open, lush and loose, spilling their fragrance, old irises from these green hills, their gnarled roots borne from house to house, from garden to garden, down through time. An iris is forever young because it has no stories to sadden it, to weigh it down.

Before me I see the violet ones, the blue ones, the yellow, the brown, and the silky white ones marked with blue, the salmon-colored ones, the coral and pink. They began their journey long before I was born, and a hundred years ago my grandmother's mother, Dorothea Morarend, seated on her front stoop just a mile from where the old man and I look down upon the river, waited for them with the same anticipation that I feel today. And yet the irises are oblivious of me and my family, are indifferent as the whitewashed boulders along that long ago driveway, stones that turned their backs to my Uncle Elvy as he dragged his sack of fish into the yard at twilight. An iris offers its beauty and fragrance as if nothing has changed, as if no one were gone.